✐ **W9-BDV-471**

AWESOME ATHLETES

YAO MING

Lydia Pyle

ABDO Publishing Company

3·07
23.00

visit us at
www.abdopub.com

Published by ABDO Publishing Company, 4940 Viking Drive, Edina, Minnesota 55435.
Copyright © 2004 by Abdo Consulting Group, Inc. International copyrights reserved in all
countries. No part of this book may be reproduced in any form without written permission from
the publisher.

Printed in the United States.

Cover Photo: PPP, Inc.
Interior Photos: Corbis pp. 8, 9, 11, 13, 14, 15, 17, 19, 20, 24, 25, 31; *Sports Illustrated* pp. 5, 10,
    15, 21, 22, 23, 26, 27, 29

Editor: Tamara L. Britton
Art Direction: Jessica A. Klein

Library of Congress Cataloging-in-Publication Data

Pyle, Lydia, 1972-
    Yao Ming / Lydia Pyle.
        p. cm. -- (Awesome athletes)
    Includes index.
    Summary: A biography of Yao Ming, the Chinese basketball player who is a star with the
Houston Rockets.
    ISBN 1-59197-484-4
    1. Ming, Yao, 1980---Juvenile literature. 2. Basketball players--China--Biography--Juvenile
literature. [1. Ming, Yao, 1980- 2. Basketball players.] I. Title. II. Series.

GV884.M558P95 2003
796.323'092--dc21
[B]   2003048132

Contents

Yao Ming

Yao Ming is the talk of the **National Basketball Association (NBA)**. The seven-foot, five-inch 22-year-old center from China has become a popular sight on and off the court. The Houston Rockets chose Yao as the number one **draft** pick in 2002. Since then, his world has moved into high gear.

Since Yao joined the Rockets, ticket sales to Asian groups have risen dramatically. Yao is also popular on the road. When Yao and the Rockets travel to other cities, 4,000 more people than normal fill the opponent's stands. Yao is also admired in his home country of China. Between 5 and 10 million people regularly tune in to watch his games on television.

Yao lives in Houston with his parents. Yao's **translator**, Colin Pine, lives with the family. Pine used to work for the U.S. government as a translator. Because Yao speaks **Mandarin** and only some English, he communicates to the media through Pine. Yao says he enjoys video games, action movies, and Starbucks.

Opposite page: Yao goes for the basket.

Growing Up in China

On September 12, 1980, Fang Feng Di and Yao Zhi Yuan welcomed their only child into the world. They named him Yao Ming. Yao was born in Shanghai, China. Baby Yao became one of the 1.3 billion people living in the world's most populous nation.

Shanghai is the largest city in China. Its population is nearly 16 million people. It is a city rich in culture and history. Shanghai is located on the East China Sea and is one of the world's largest seaports.

When Yao was born, he was almost two feet long. But this was not surprising, since both his parents are tall. Yao's mother is six feet, three inches tall and is a former captain of the Chinese national basketball team. His father is six feet, seven inches tall and is also a former basketball player.

When Yao was four years old, he had to buy an adult ticket to ride the bus because he was

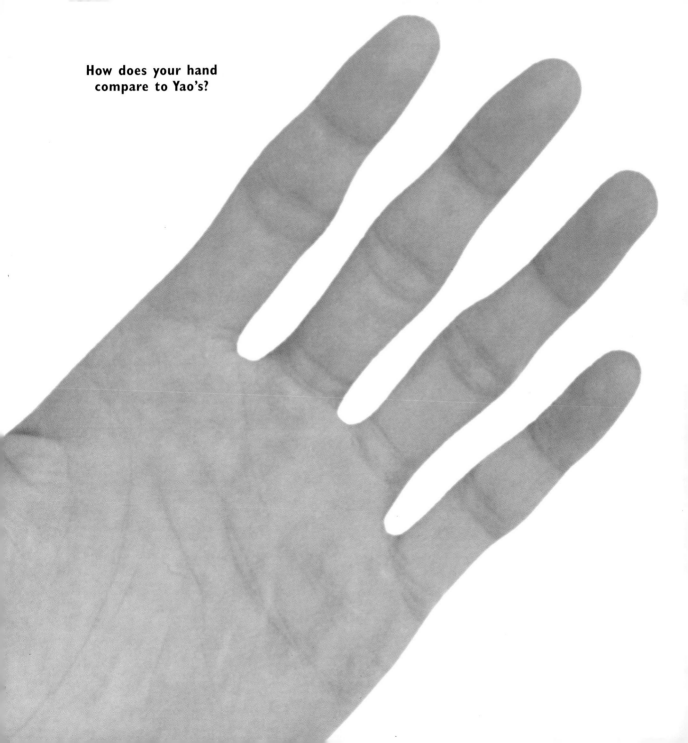

How does your hand
compare to Yao's?

so tall. He was taller than his elementary school teacher. By the time Yao was a teenager, he was seven feet tall. Yao had to sleep diagonally on a king-size bed. His clothes were specially ordered to fit his large size.

When Yao was 13 years old, his parents sent him to a sports academy in Shanghai. Yao spent several hours a day practicing basketball. It was here that Yao developed a passion for the game.

But it was not always like that. When Yao was nine, his first basketball coach remembers that Yao did not like basketball much, and that he was only able to run four laps around the court!

Yao towers over the other athletes at the Asian Games in Pusan, South Korea.

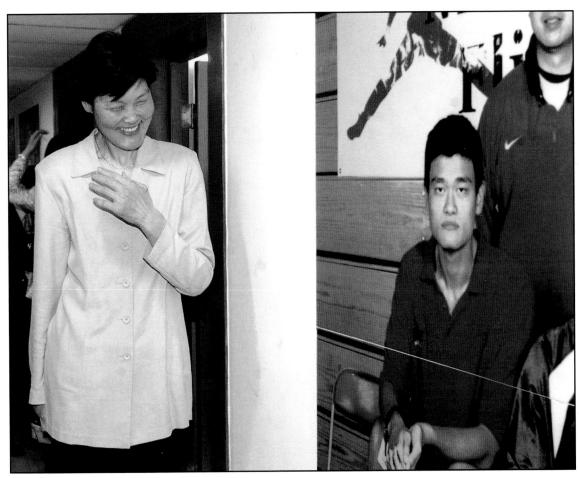

Yao's mother, Fang Feng Di, looks at a poster of Yao in Shanghai.

Playing Basketball in China

Yao began playing for the Shanghai Sharks basketball team in 1997. That year he also attended a Nike basketball camp in Paris. Del Harris, then the coach of the Los Angeles Lakers, saw Yao at the camp and said, "I gotta get a picture with that kid because one day he's gonna have a real impact in the **NBA**."

Yao became well known during his five-year career with the Shanghai Sharks. While playing with the Sharks, he also played on the Chinese Junior National Team and the Chinese National Team.

Left and opposite page: Yao plays with the Chinese National Team.

The Chinese National Team played Qatar in 1998. In that game, Yao had 17 blocks. Yao also played for China in the 2000 Olympics in Sydney, Australia. China's Olympic team came in 10th out of 12 teams.

Yao led the Sharks to the **Chinese Basketball Association (CBA)** title in 2002. Then the Chinese National Team played Team USA on August 22, 2002. Though Yao scored 13 points and had 11 rebounds, Team USA beat China 84-54. After playing against Yao, Boston Celtic Paul Pierce said, "He's very fundamentally sound for a guy his size. He's got a soft touch. He can run the floor and is very **agile**."

Yao's career average in the CBA was 23.4 points and 15.4 rebounds per game. He averaged 32.4 points, 19 rebounds, and 4.8 blocked shots a game during his last season.

Just before Yao came to the United States to play for the Houston Rockets, he competed in the Asian Games with the Chinese National Team. They lost the championship game to South Korea and received the silver medal. Yao scored 23 points and had 22 rebounds in the game.

Opposite page: New Zealand's Sean Marks blocks a shot attempt by Yao at the 2000 summer Olympic Games.

THE MAKING OF AN AWESOME ATHLETE

Yao is one of the tallest players in the NBA today.

1980	1997	1998	2000
Born September 12 in Shanghai, China	Becomes a member of the Shanghai Sharks	Has 17 blocks in a game against Qatar	Plays for China in the Olympic Games in Sydney, Australia

How Awesome Is He?

See how Yao's career averages measure up to those of some of the NBA's tallest players.

Player	Height	PPG	RPG
Manute Bol	7'7"	2.6	4.2
Gheorghe Muresan	7'7"	9.8	6.4
Shawn Bradley	7'6"	9.3	7.2
Yao Ming	**7'5"**	**13.8**	**8.3**
Zydrunas Ilgauskas	7'3"	13.9	7.4
Arvydas Sabonis	7'3"	12.2	7.4
Dikembe Mutombo	7'2"	12.3	12.2

YAO MING

TEAM: HOUSTON ROCKETS
NUMBER: 11
POSITION: CENTER
HEIGHT: 7 FEET, 5 INCHES
WEIGHT: 296 POUNDS

2002	2002	2002	2003
Leads Shanghai Sharks to CBA championship title	Drafted number one by the Houston Rockets	Is December's NBA Rookie of the Month	Becomes first Asian player to start in an NBA All-Star Game

- Was the CBA's Most Valuable Player in 2001
- Was on China's World Championship team in 2002
- Scored NBA career high 30 points on November 27, 2002
- Had NBA career high 18 rebounds on December 1, 2002

Highlights

The 2002 NBA Draft

There was lots of talk leading up to the 2002 **NBA draft**. Was China going to allow Yao to play in the United States? Which team would select him? Many teams were interested in Yao. The Chicago Bulls and the New York Knicks had private workouts with Yao. He also participated in a workout at Loyola University that included representatives from 25 teams.

Chinese government officials were cautious about letting Yao play in the United States. They wanted to know what city he would play in. They wanted to make sure it had a strong Asian community. They also wanted to know how much money he was going to make. Yao is a national treasure in China, and they wanted to make sure he would not embarrass the Chinese people by playing in the NBA.

Yao speaks with reporters the day after being drafted number one by the Houston Rockets.

Once the Chinese government learned that the Rockets had the first pick in the **draft** and that they wanted Yao, it was a go. On June 26, 2002, Yao was drafted number one by the Houston Rockets. He became the tallest player ever selected first in the draft. He is also the first foreign player to be picked number one without having played for a college in the United States.

Yao signed a four-year, $17.8 million contract with the Rockets. "It's a new beginning for me. American basketball has its own unique culture. I hope I can adapt quickly," Yao said about playing in the **NBA**.

Yao's contract took months to negotiate. In the end, the Houston Rockets had to pay the Shanghai Sharks $350,000 for the rights to Yao. Yao has to pay the Chinese government half of his earnings, including **endorsement** deals. Yao will still play in national and international events for China, and the Rockets will have Yao for all regular season and playoff games.

Yao bids farewell to his parents.

A Houston Rocket

Because of Yao's commitments to the Chinese National Team, he arrived in Houston late. Yao joined his team in late October 2002, just nine days before the **NBA**'s season opener. "In the first practice, we could see that he had a lot of skill," said Maurice Taylor, a forward for the Rockets, "but he was lost. Brand-new system, brand-new rules, he was a **rookie**."

Yao made his NBA debut during a preseason game against the San Antonio Spurs on October 23, 2002. Yao played for 13 minutes and had six points, four rebounds, four fouls, and three turnovers. "I haven't had many guys make me feel short," said Spurs center David Robinson, "he made me feel short and small."

Yao is guarded by Kevin Willis in a game against the Spurs.

Yao had a rough start to the season, averaging only four points in the first six games. It was easy to see that Yao was a bit confused and often out of position.

But, Yao began playing better and showing off his talents from late November into December. He was nine for nine in shooting and scored 20 points against the Los Angeles Lakers on November 18, 2002.

Yao started in his first **NBA** game on November 22, 2002, against the Washington Wizards. He

Yao splits the Laker D and goes in for the dunk!

scored 18 points and had four blocked shots in a 93-86 win. He was the NBA's Western Conference got milk? **Rookie** of the Month in December 2002.

On January 17, 2003, the Rockets and Lakers met up again. Yao blocked Shaquille O'Neal's first three shots and made a huge dunk with 10 seconds left to help win in overtime. By late January 2003, Yao was averaging 13 points and eight rebounds per game.

Yao guards Shaquille O'Neal.

Yao goes in for a layup.

An All-Star

In late January 2003, Yao was chosen by fans to start in the **NBA** All-Star Game for the Western Conference. He beat out Shaquille O'Neal for starting center by almost 250,000 votes! A **rookie** hadn't been voted to start in an All-Star Game since Grant Hill in 1995. Yao became the fourth rookie center to start in an All-Star Game. "I am honored. I hope to play well in the game," Yao said.

The All-Star Game was played on February 9, 2003, in Atlanta, Georgia. The day before the big game, Yao drew a large crowd of media. More than 120 journalists, reporters, and television crews from around the world crowded together to hear what Yao had to say.

Yao listens to a question from a reporter during the All-Star media event.

When Yao walked in he was wearing his Chinese National Team jersey. "It's to show I really miss my audience, my family and friends back in China," Yao said.

"This is really special. I still think the greatest excitement is to be selected to the All-Star team. Nothing can be more exciting than that," Yao said during the media event. When Shaquille O'Neal was asked about Yao he said, "A guy like Yao Ming is good for the game. He's a new face, an exciting face. He's a good guy."

Kobe Bryant guards teammate Yao during practice for the All-Star Game.

Yao became the first Asian player ever to start in an **NBA** All-Star Game. He played 17 minutes and had two points and two rebounds. Yao's Western Conference beat the Eastern Conference 155-145 in double overtime. "I just sit back and enjoy the game, because the whole game, for me, is a fun place," Yao said.

Coach Rudy Tomjanovich discusses a play with Yao.

Shaquille O'Neal guards Yao.

A Popular Guy

Yao Ming has become a household name in the United States. His big smile and sense of humor have drawn many people to him. He has appeared on the cover of *Sports Illustrated* three times already. There is even a song written about him. Chance McClain and Kevin Ryan wrote "It's a Ming Thing." It is often heard before Yao's **NBA** games.

Yao has appeared in two major television commercials. He was seen in an Apple computer commercial along with Verne Troyer, who played Mini-Me in the Austin Powers movies. Yao was also in a Visa commercial that first aired on Super Bowl Sunday. That is just the beginning of **endorsements** for Yao. He will soon appear in ads for Gatorade, China Unicom, and Sorent.

Yao has opened up the market for sports apparel in Asia. New NBA-licensed clothing makes its debut in China in April 2003. Among the clothes will be a signature Yao Ming number 11 jersey.

Fan Web sites about Yao Ming have been popping up in both English and **Mandarin**. The Yao Ming Fan Club is also growing each day. People around the world are intrigued by the seven-foot, five-inch gentle giant from China.

Yao is surrounded by young Rockets fans.

Glossary

agile - able to move with ease.

Chinese Basketball Association (CBA) - a professional basketball league in China.

draft - an event during which NBA teams choose amateur players to play on their team.

endorsement - allowing a company to use your name and image to sell a product in exchange for money.

Mandarin - the main language of the Chinese people.

National Basketball Association (NBA) - a professional basketball league in the United States and Canada consisting of the Eastern and Western Conferences.

rookie - a first-year player in a professional sports league.

translator - someone who takes words from one language and puts them into another language.

Web Sites

To learn more about Yao Ming, visit ABDO Publishing Company on the World Wide Web at **www.abdopub.com**. Web sites about Yao Ming are featured on our Book Links page. These links are routinely monitored and updated to provide the most current information available.

Index